Wolf Devouring a Wolf Devouring a Wolf

I0625558

Wolf Devouring a Wolf Devouring a Wolf

Cassandra Whitaker

JACKLEG PRESS

JackLeg Press

www.jacklegpress.org

Copyright © 2025 by Cassandra Whitaker.

Published 2025 by JackLeg Press. All rights reserved.

Printed in the United States of America.

ISBN: 978-1956907186

No part of this work may be reproduced or utilized in any form or by any means, electronic or mechanical, including microfilm, photocopying, and recording, or by any information storage and retrieval system, without permission in writing from the publisher.

Library of Congress Control Number: 2023945762

Cover art: francescoch

Praise for Casandra Whitaker's Work

Cassandra Whitaker's *Wolf Devouring a Wolf Devouring a Wolf* is indulgent, showing us that everything is connected. Through its use of contrapuntal, the metaphor of a wolf, portraiture, song, repetition, and fragmentation, it cycles through thoughts—about family, gender-based violence, transformation, emptiness—to refine those thoughts and invites readers to do the same. Through this book, I've come to know more about the wolf inside the speaker, their mom, dad, lovers, and myself. Through reading this, I've relearned what it means to be an active participant—in the act of poetry and life.
—KB Brookins, author of *Pretty*

In a series of engagements with the figure of the wolf, Cassandra Whitaker's *Wolf Devouring a Wolf Devouring a Wolf* moves beyond the usual conceit of wolf-as-predator, crafting a fairy-tale like exploration of masculinity, dysphoria, chronic emptiness, and violence. Rather than taking narrative form, Whitaker's work utilizes the rhythms and brevity of song—more lullaby than Grimms—utilizing a verse that unfurls, canon-like, into sustained recitatives. On the page, this takes the form of serial poems, diagrams, contrapuntals, antiphonal lyrics. Whitaker's use of repetition, revision, and mid-poem revelation stand out: The wolf swallowed me / up, one bite at a time, she writes—No. The wolf /swallowed me over /and over/again. // No. I lived / in its jaws. Ultimately, *Wolf Devouring a Wolf Devouring a Wolf*'s movement is not toward a critique but understanding, growth, recovery. What is it to be devoured in failing to devour? She asks and answers for us: I, in the mouth of the wolf / wanting to be devoured? Which is love.
 —Jos Charles, author of *a Year & other poems*

Cassandra Whitaker's *Wolf Devouring a Wolf Devouring a Wolf* amazes with its ferocity, subtlety, and sheer originality. With startling fervor, these poems portray and embody the agonies and triumphs of living one's primary truth. Like no other poet, Whitaker attends to the liminal spaces between self and family, wildness and culture, freedom and necessity. Contemporary poetry is richer and deeper for this astonishing collection.

—Peter Campion, author of *Radical as Reality: Form and Freedom in American Poetry*

Cassandra Whitaker's debut collection *Wolf Devouring a Wolf Devouring a Wolf* is a relapsing memory. And just as memories rewrite themselves over time, this collection revises how we remember ourselves in family dynamics. This collection is interrogation "on the space between emptiness" through repetition, visualization, splitting of the page, and personification of the wolf (the tyrannical parent, the unfit caregiver). Every step we take with these poems brings us inches closer to the jaws of the wolf.

—jason b. crawford, author of *Year of the Unicorn Kidz*

Cassandra Whitaker's *Wolf Devouring a Wolf Devouring a Wolf* is a recursive, queer tale of transformation. Vulnerable and fierce, dual and singular, the wolf is external, the wolf is internal, the wolf is dynamic. Whitaker's powerful, formally innovative poems present a harrowing journey and reach the apogee of realized joy. 'I am I am I am the oldest answer the moon knows.'

—Suzanne Frischkorn, author of *Whipsaw*

"The wolf announces all worth," Cassandra Whitaker writes in *A Wolf Devouring a Wolf Devouring a Wolf*, "with his saddest syllable." This book is many things, including a new script to recast an old fairy tale, a way of re-diagraming what family and love can mean, a tool to reveal the wolf in language's clothing, a suture for the wound. "My voice sings back," Whitaker writes in one wise poem and adds in another, "a chorus humming—*here*—*here*—*find us/* here A body— a door." In *A Wolf Devouring a Wolf Devouring a Wolf*, Cassandra Whitaker has given us a doorway that leads into astonishment. She has written unforgettable and necessary book.

—James Allen Hall, author of *Romantic Comedy*, & co-host of the podcast *Breaking Form*

Contents

The Wolf Lent Me My Name, 1

Diagram Of Mother, 2

Floor Plan, 3

Wolf Territory, 5

Halloween With The Wolf, 7

Family, 8

What Shall The Wolf Sing?, 9

Pattern Of Family Migration, 11

Diagram of Father, 12

Wolf Moves In The Shape, 13

Growing Up In The Mouth Of The Wolf, 14

Shelter Of The Wolf, 16

Wolf In Dark Elms, 17

Under The Influence Of The Moon, 18

Diagram Of Desire, 20

What Claims Wolves Laid   Upon My Body, 21

Wolf Appeared   For Me, 22

The Wolf's House In The Early Morning, 23

How I Could Not Quit The Wolf, 24

With the Wolf— Again— After Many Weeks, 25

What Wolf—That Kissed Me So—, 26

The Wolf—I Should Have Known, 27

Wolf Promise Of Love, 28

Self Portrait, 30

Interior, 31

For the Wolf—I Left, 32

The Wolf Eats, 33

Take One Mouth And Consume The Mouth of Another, 34

Stretch The Wolf's Mouth, 35

I Hear The Wolf Outside, 36

Wrestling Wolves, 37

Wolf Comes To—Early Morning, 40

I Am The Wolf's Unending Meal, 41

Hunted, 42

I Met The Wolf Halfway, 43

The Inside of a Wolf, 44

Mirror The Wolf, 45

Wrestling With The Wolf, 46

A Wolf Devours A Wolf Devours A Wolf, 47

I Make A Roof Out Of The Wolf, 48

In Some Southern Village, 49

Diagram Of Transformation, 50

Wolf In The Meadow, 51

Wolf Who Is Not A Wolf Plays In The Forest, 52

Inside The Hollow Is A Song, 54

Noctivagant, 55

Wolves Prop Up The Moon   They Gather—Rhyming, 57

Swallowed By The Wolf, 58

Emptiness Sestina, 60

What The Wolf Fears, 61

On The Four Corners Of The World, 62

Pelt Of The Wolf, 63

I Dress the Wolf in Flowers, 67

Acknowledgments, 69

The wolf is the first to tell you there is no wolf

The Wolf Lent Me My Name

and my name lent me shelter

from the wolf and the emptiness that the wolf lent me

Emptiness—a hide that hid me—

carried me through emptiness

which the wolf lent me — worn until it could not be worn

— emptiness— the wearing—

the filling— pretending emptiness—

emptiness is not what fills the emptiness inside

the name which the wolf lent me

Diagram Of Mother

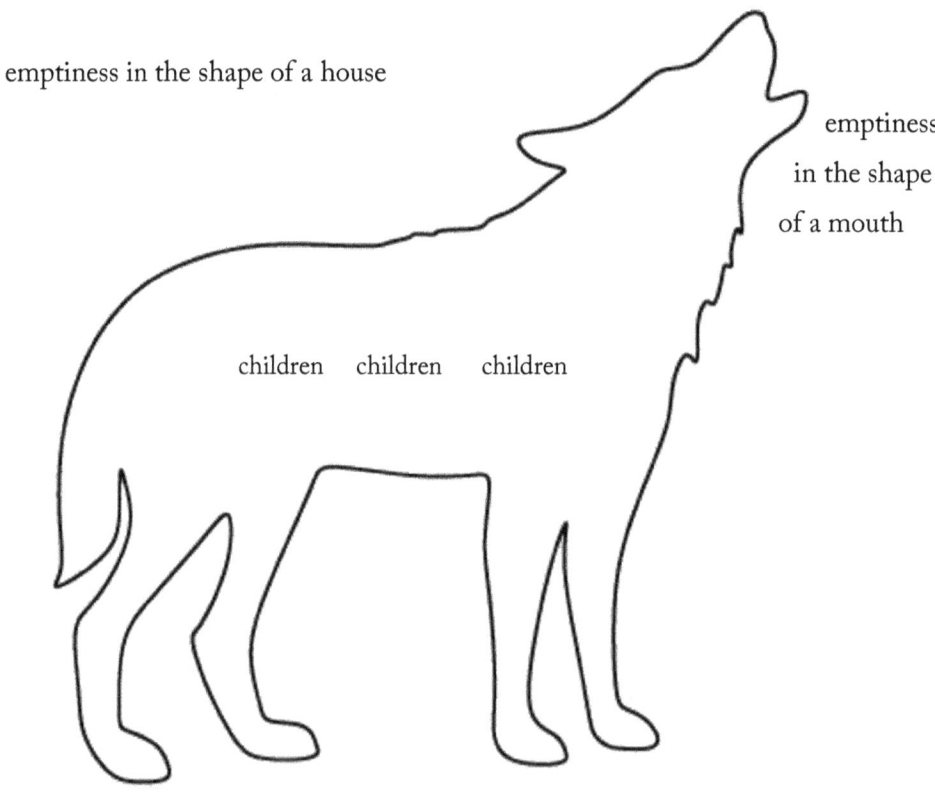

Father's absence

emptiness in the shape of a house

emptiness
in the shape
of a mouth

children   children   children

a mother's love   a mother's love   a mother's love   a mother's love

Floor Plan

Wolf is in the house
The house is

                                         in the wolf   The wolf
                                                is the house

The wolf
is the house   The wolf

                                           makes a house
                                           for the house

a house of emptiness
Emptiness is not

                                           made less
                            empty   The house increases

emptiness by adding
home

                                           A home
                        in emptiness   A home made

of emptiness
What is a house

                                    empty of home? A wolf?

                                                        A wolf's wolf

want? The wolf

is in the house   The house

                                                  in the wolf The wolf builds

                                                                    a house

out of emptiness   Emptiness

in a home is a wolf

Wolf Territory

Once I went to play / outside with my friends— girls / and we turned circles and pretended / to blast bullets off our bracelets We swirled / in the front lawn— we / twirled / until my mother interrupted—her shocked face / her urgent and strident reprimands That pointed finger / passing through my body / and into my body's memory / and into my brain poking and pulling apart / whatever it did not like

The wolf grinding away / at flesh / My mother's twisted sense / of a body passed into my body / It has passed through / my body It has passed / I remember /

once—how upset she was— wearing shorts / entering the grocery store / with her baby—me / I understood what she said Her thighs / were fat and awful How ashamed / she should be / for being so   I remember / not knowing how to say I love / you I remember wanting / to hold on to her / slender neck The curious / look I gave people in the grocery store / as if they were going gnash my mother's body / for being a body

The wolf grinding / away at flesh

A body is full / of secrets   Secrets swell / take on weight—gravity / pressurize the body

For a while I found boyhood / wore it like a costume / spoke to it—nourished it / the costume—because (the wolf) / I hated my (the wolf's) body / How I learned to hide / my body— each cut / each bruise / each needle mark—all / that I assumed I wore / a body like a costume / I wore a costume / like a person

I hate the way your body makes me / feel My mother's body imposed upon my body / how could I not feel / the wolf grinding away at flesh?

With the emptiness inside I am / full I put the wolf outside myself / and fill up the emptiness / inside   I put the wolf out

Halloween With The Wolf

After returning home I took off my Wonder / Woman costume—which wasn't even my costume / I just pretended it was because I had to / wear a Batman costume because I was a boy / and not Wonder Woman in search of a girl / to inspire At home— later— at the coffee table / in the same room where my mother nearly died—where I watched / Wonder Woman— which was the moon rising / in the living room Little me unwrapped candy—one at a time / and chewed / not understanding the delight / I felt was delight at being eaten by the wolf / chocolate after chocolate / already starting to hate what I was— a body / in service to mother in service to father who only prayed to the moon / while the wolf ate and ate—each bite / replacing my emptiness with the wolf's emptiness / one bite at a time—consumed by the want of love My mother / did not watch while the wolf ate me and ate me / What did I not understand? / The wolf had eaten her words / The wolf had hollowed her out / from within

Family

The wolf told me   I was good enough
just sitting there   in her jaw
open to whatever pleasures she desired—   I gave her everything—
if only she would love   me

What didn't I understand?

When?

I was better

When?

I could have left the wolf—but didn't

What Shall The Wolf Sing?

The wolf shames me for watching   my own border

The moon steals everything   it owns No wonder

the wolf follows—   the wolf leaves tracks

    There is so much joy in fleshing

    The wolf doesn't mind its own trail

    The wolf—she sings

When you own the earth   *with your feet and mouth*

there is no hour but now—now   *Is there another way*

to love one completely—   *to return them home*

    the hollow hollow of my ache?

    My ache—

    the gain of want

On words—   the wolf turned the moment into

a fleshing The wolf carries away   a piece of joy—where the wolf fleshed

flesh out of love   Out of love— the fiercest wolves appear—

9

I hate your body
and how your body makes me
feel Your body—Mine

Pattern Of Family Migration

The wolf raised the ceiling and howled over it
The wolf raised the prey and gobbled under it

                    The wolf lied to the child and dug under it
                    The wolf lied to the moon and doubled under it

The wolf devoured a wolf and muted it
The wolf capped a lie with a lie and stole it

                    The wolf ate a wolf with a wolf and loved it
                    The wolf desired flesh to unflesh it

The wolf starved a wolf and loved it
The wolf loved a wolf and ate it

Diagram of Father

this Mine This Is mine is mine is mine Mine This This IS Mine Mine this IS mine
This— this This is mine this is mine this is mine this is mine this is mine   this is mine this
is mine Is mine is mine is mine is This is Mine This is mine   this is mine
This Is   Mine This is Mine Mine This Is Mine This   This Is
Mine THIS IS MINE THIS is mine this—mine this–   mine This Is
Mine This— mine Mine MINE MINE   MINE This is
this is mine This is this   is this is is mine
Mine mine mine   mine mine MINE
THIS— THIS   THIS MINE mine
MINE THIS   this IS mine— this
THIS is mine   mine This is mine this
is mine this is   mine is   mine is mine this is
MINE this is   MINE this is   mine this is mine this is
mine this is mine   This—mine mine   mine This Is Mine Is
mine is mine   mine   this is MINE   This IS MINE—this Mine
Mine Mine Mine   Is   MINE is   mine is mine is mine is
mine THIS Is   Mine   Mine mine mine this Is   Mine mine mine mine

12

Wolf Moves In The Shape

of hunger in the shape of hunger   a ring of forest

a wolf moves and circles back   sings

to deer—where they lay   the forest song all about growing

clover lorn—the wolf   nursing a hum

rings town like the moon   to up up up the young

backs his kind   into crowns

the mind of the packs   and canopies

converge here—along the river   for bird minds and butterfly minds

and the stores by the river   and all thoughts of sunny—over and over

and the banks by the river   and over the thought—green

and the schools   up and through the forest

by the river   pines the wolf counting

hunger—under coin's invisible power   what is mine and mine

a god to wolf—the power   is hunger stretching its mouth out

in the shape of a moon   is green reaching out—mine

in the shape of belly in the shape of a town   mine—mine

with money packed like teeth in the mouth   circles like the circle of thought

shaped from a wolf's hunger—extending out   in the mind—What is this?

Hunger is never out   —mine What is this? Mine

Growing Up In The Mouth Of The Wolf

By age three men terrified / me—I have picked up / this bone and chewed on it—gnawed / on it I remember being / powerless— alone / in the dark / with men I remember / men whispering / into my ear— *it's going to be alright* A man / holding onto all body / to keep me still / A man handed me a shotgun / a pistol / a rifle / Then held me down / so I wouldn't feel the recoil / my body blown back / my eyes empty / of all

Firearms enforce the wolf's freedom A boy / must learn to be / a wolf / The wolf swallowed me Men / of my childhood hated They ate / with their eyes The wolf swallowed me / up— one bite at a time

No The wolf / swallowed me over / and over / again

No I lived / in its jaws Let it chew / on flesh—mind The wolf / fear The white / Wolf The wolf / Father

Father claims / he moved / his family to Virginia / in the middle of the night / so his children would not grow up / around a culture of killing—where killing / is the groom It's taken years to strip / away fur and teeth My father's own / kingdom—steepled—a soft / cruelty My father

/ —in his own way— was only removed / from the pack—but not free / from the moon's influence

The moon requires / blood from all wolves / I did not / belong in my family / but it was clear I belonged / to my family—a thing to be shaped and shamed / and shamed and raised up / into what? A what? A wolf

Shelter Of The Wolf

Shelter / Of the wolf / Shelter— still Shelter / of money / love The wolf demands / obedience / Shelter / Against teeth Against / all wind / and wind's wind / change

To the moon / all must be / given up—love / a body— a mind / Pups given up / flesh for fleshing / Shelter fed / polished / to a sheen / shelter sheltered me / Would I have lived? / Outside?

When I put / the wolf outside / myself I found / myself without / a throat / the moon / shuttered by pine / shatters Malice / would have fleshed / me— wore me— / my emptiness filled / with emptiness bluster

The wolf / raised me to flesh
A wolf / sheltered me / from wolves

16

Wolf In Dark Elms

Moon preaches   flesh

on flesh   on bone

rush— preaching pack and   pack and pack—

how everything belongs   to the moon

Even lone wolves are intrigued   by the promise of belonging

to the moon hanging   in sanctuary elms

like a thought that's just been thought   —the moon follows

all night   like a great idea

Hunger comes in on its knees   Pray to emptiness— pray

to silence Hunger answers   every hour— every minute— every second

— every utterance— every appetite—   answered—

answered double *I am I am*   *I hunger I hunger*

17

Under The Influence Of The Moon

Wolf expects / to serve with all breath With all breath / the wolf will rise out of death / and begin again to flesh / what it wishes / All the wolf desires / to rise above / The chorus? Mine— mine— do you hear?

*

Wolf's teeth rip   for the moon's influence—hungry

for more influence—   for more light—let in every time

the wolf rends flesh   for flesh for flesh Flesh is plentiful

Earth has made so much flesh   It is the one thing

emptiness never tires of—flesh   It is more plentiful than ever before—flesh

Emptiness covers—smothers—assumes   The wolf—a kind of frontier

Emptiness   —this vastness to be filled

*

The wolf is the first

to tell you there is no wolf in the forest

The wolf sings   his hymn

I swallowed him up

                                       I swallowed him up

                —from the foot

        to the crown of his bald top—   *I swallowed him up I did*

                                    —I swallowed him up

*

Worship began / as worth ship / the condition/ of being worthy Is that why / no flesh is turned/ away? The wolf announces all worth/ with his saddest syllable It becomes cherished / After so much blood / after so much / loss It becomes cherished

The moon is no fool / she borrows her happiness every night The wolf cannot/ tell The wolf believes the lie It is all / the wolf can carve Out/ of emptiness he eclipses want

 Who will cover the land/ with want? Who will leave/ the forest wanting?

Diagram Of Desire

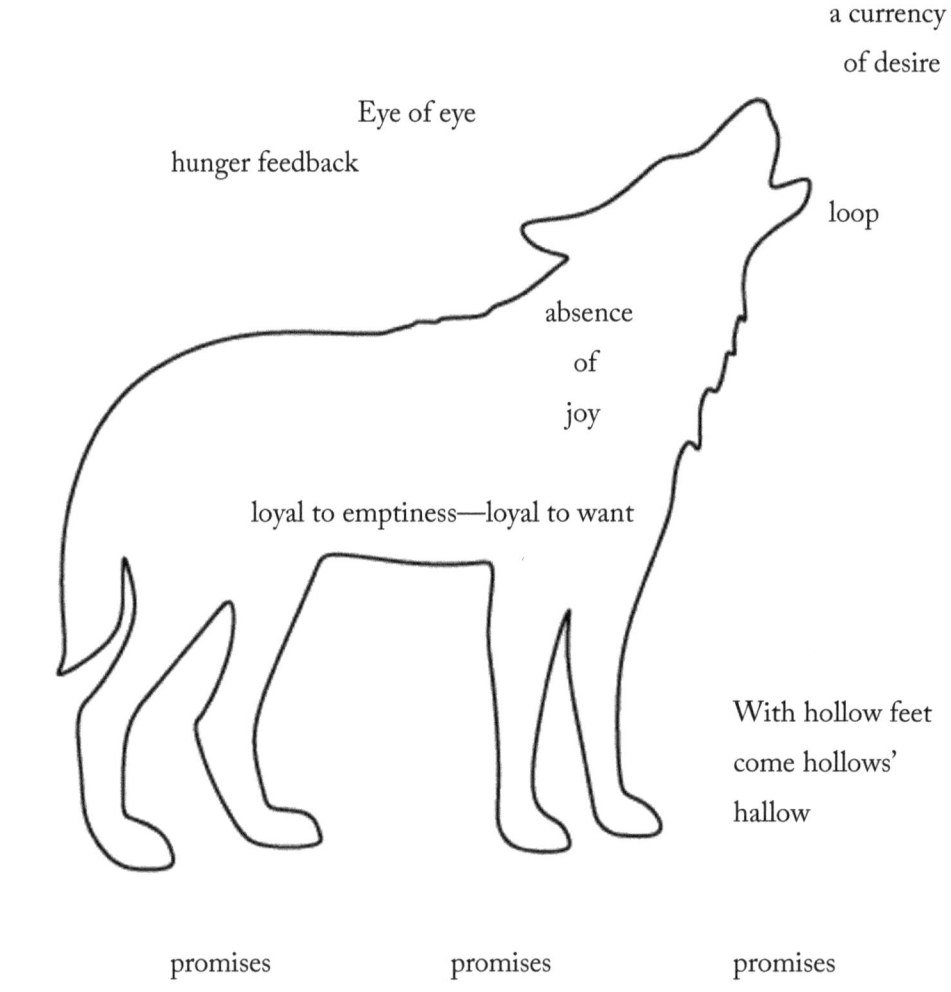

a currency
of desire

Eye of eye

hunger feedback

loop

absence
of
joy

loyal to emptiness—loyal to want

With hollow feet
come hollows'
hallow

promises   promises   promises   promises

What Claims Wolves Laid   Upon My Body

that summer so weird   so hot—thick with youth
one boy after another   I could hardly stay
in one place—one foot   departing before
arriving—one hand in   the exit—one hand warm
one cooling grip—mouth   learning one lesson
upon the body   eager for more more
the way urge begets   the urge—emptiness
a child—more—more—more   doubling desire
how a fire chooses   love's love—air—air—breath
the quickness of wolves   restricting my throat
where wolves fleshed flesh   unlearning all green growth
which grew me even   in pain—more and more
under oaks—under dark   wolves claimed me

Wolf Appeared   For Me

in the gloom | before our dark meeting

in the back of some bushed road | overgrow with memories

—memories' emptiness | among aluminum cans

crushed cigarettes —wet paper sacks | some Saturday night

let loose from its host — the bag | as ruined as I ever was with the wolf

who might as well have stolen me from home | With want taking me—

the wolf revealed my emptiness | what emptiness looks like

when it gazes upon itself | in secret or in pain or howling

again | —again—again

The Wolf's House In The Early Morning

I left	out the back the way
I came	and into the forest
—slipped like a thought and remembered	my good name
from whence I came which was	far away
—bloodless—	tame

How I Could Not Quit The Wolf

I—   in the mouth of the wolf—

wanting   to be devoured?

Which is

love Only I could feed   the wolf's emptiness—

only I could pretend I wasn't   as empty—or as hungry

Only I could feed

the wolf this way   —this hour—a passing pleasure

behind the teeth   of the wolf's glamour — a song — a bait

—a lie   —want—wanting

With the Wolf—Again—After Many Weeks

Together   we packed

our desires   into our desires—

multiplied   our pleasure

into each other   and into each other furred

and gnawed   and chased

anger   to the moon and returned to feast and feast

and left emptiness emptiness   at our feet

What Wolf—That Kissed Me So—

                        in kissing   me

    kissed himself—together we fell into   a single pleasure

            the wolf and I He—pressing   my kisses

into his emptiness saying do and do and do—   the wolf

        whispering into my ear—which was   his ear

    that afternoon in the dark apartment   over the ache

        that was the village The village—   our careless care

            open like a song is open—   ready to be

            quickened to chorus—then left   alone

        to finish its breath Breath was all   he wanted—

    was all he gave—leaving me—which was   himself—

    singing alone in the village emptiness—   which was mine

The Wolf—I Should Have Known

He locked on me / when we matched / eyes Our bright blue mirrors revealed / desire In minutes / I / softening his warmth / He wouldn't let my hands touch / him He hooked / my mouth / He followed me / I grew wise to his shadow / He led me / In parking lot darkness / He would not allow me / to touch him I revealed truth / with my mouth / He would not kiss me He held me apart / I grew wise to his shadow / He folded darkness like a page / He led me / into the story of desire / I heard but could not see / When he left me / the woods wheeled wild with stars

Wolf Promise Of Love

Wolf says forever by ripping flesh into emptiness
by calling out the answer to the moon's riddles
I am I am I am the oldest answer the moon knows
but does not understand

The moon borrows everything
The wolf takes everything One is the shade
of the other

Wolf promises forever
by gobbling up flesh to fill emptiness
Wolf promises and promises and promises Forever is farther
Forever is a notion between the sun
and the moon

The moon prefers singing
the slippery now

This is how I am
tonight *This is how I am tonight*
Take me or do not *take me how I am*
Tonight

In the wolf's promise—teeth

as bare as moonrock   In the wolf's promise—a lie

a truth—the now is   never

Self Portrait

Want like the moon—

To accelerate emptiness by feeding

emptiness itself—a drink—

a shot—a lie

accelerating

a desire to eat itself

a mouth
devouring
a mouth

Something is wrong — wrong

there is something wrong—wrong

with my body—mine

You are not   you are not   you are naught   you are a knot of want

Interior

The wolf eats you
The wolf eats you
The wolf eats you

> You shout at the center of emptiness
> Shouting at the center
> Emptiness upon the heart like a glove

The wolf eats you
The wolf eats you
The wolf eats you

> A voice cries out in the wilderness
> A voice cries out
> You shout at the center of emptiness

For the Wolf—I Left

For AS

I left my brother   for the wolf—a hundred in guilty
numbers—some errant want to be alone

I left my mother   for the wolf to leave the wolf full of
borrowed mother

I left my father   for the wolf and watched the wolf return to
eat joy like a word salad

I left my teacher   for the wolf and found myself holding up
the wolf's words with my own

I left my god   for the wolf and found a wolf waiting on
emptiness to empty itself

I left god   for the wolf and discovered my emptiness

I left my emptiness   for the wolf and uncovered a hole

I left my mind   for the wolf to unlearn time

I left my wolf   for emptiness and filled it with glamor

I left my wolf   for glamor and filled the wolf with
emptiness

The Wolf Eats

When the full moon asks—   the wolf turns its emptiness inside out—
    the wolf fills up   the moon inside the belly

Flesh is plentiful
The earth has made so much
flesh It is the one thing
emptiness does not tire of—flesh
It is not precious It is not
precious—flesh It is more plentiful
than ever before—flesh
Emptiness demands
so much Emptiness requires all

The wolf listens—tracks—senses   emptied of all but emptiness
There is no end to it   Everything the wolf owns
is spent as the open open   The wolf eats and eats
'til the moon is full enough to ask for more   There is always more
It is the one song the wolf has written—   everything the wolf owns
is stolen from a mouth swallowing   a mouth swallowing a mouth

Take One Mouth And Consume The Mouth of Another

Wolves keep springing
from wolves' bodies

Out of one springs mother

Out of mother springs father

Further off a charmer sings
who turns the other way

to the moon's moon
for departure

All of the earth's worn teeth

sharpen again All of moon's pleasures
larger——larger

diminishes again All wolves grow emptiness

All wolves cry to the moon
with loneliness—
its happiness—a wolf leaves
a body of a wolf through a body of
—take one howl—rhyme it with the other
——there is a mouth that is its mother——
and another

The moon rhymes emptiness
turns away to borrow
a body of a wolf's wolf escaping
the wolf Take one tail—tie it to another
There is a mouth that needs no other—
one mouth consumes the mouth of another

34

Stretch The Wolf's Mouth

Open and fold the lower jaw
back and fold the upper jaw
back and step inside— heel first
pushing all the way into emptiness
Jump—pound— deep into the wolf
Climb in —push your arms through the forelegs
into paws The hide warm at first—
but then gripping cold as emptiness takes you In its mouth
all hope fades like an echo In its mouth
all joy fades like an echo Like an echo
all memory of what it was like— fades
until it answers no more— only a wolf remains—
a servant to emptiness

I Hear The Wolf Outside

I hear the wolf / Outside / myself the wolf / I—Hear / flesh fleshing itself / For the wolf / Unflesh all / That is / Precious /the wolf devours / The wolf / Follows / Outside Myself / I flesh / my flesh Wait / to be / Lied to / By the moon / The moon is / Empty / Of the wolf / Its truth / its happiness / Borrowed / From the sun / The wolf / Outside—I /hear / It / Hunger

Wrestling Wolves

Is there ever a moment when a wolf does not know

emptiness inside

waiting to be filled by warmth—flesh

or flesh's flesh—desire? The wolf

pleads for fragility—how flesh

is so difficult to flesh

for the moon—that the moon

keeps asking and asking and asking

going dark before showing its whole face

again—while the wolf does what?

Waits Waiting in weeds as if the wolf

is some beast and not the mouth

of god That look of the wolf

looking back—I have you

again—I have you There was never any question

—all anger remains—all anger's

anger—the wolf

reaches through space—age

I flicker

Into myself—my future happiness
chiming in—let go the dead wolf thoughts
let go the dead wolf wisdom—Falling—that noise Falling

through space The wolf glaring back at me
from behind—here I am My death
bag catch—my danger danger

Remember the misery of the body
staring at itself in the mirror
while wishing a body
was out of its body?

Invite the predator
to preach the moon's influence No one
will be listening   All will be laughing
How deflated the wolf will become

turn him
out into the pack
and make joy
out of teeth clenched
upon the throat

Or kill the wolf—gut it
to watch bodies spill out—bodies

                                        covered in the wolf's emptiness

                in each mouth more emptiness

                                        echoing the dead's joy

swallowed

with twenty-six muscles working

together to take the whole

of what it latches onto

                The echo of joy inside emptiness

                                        is a loop Will the wolf

                                        ever be

                                        full? Will the wolf ever be

                                        satisfied?

That sound you hear

It isn't a howl

Mine   Mine   Mine

Wolf Comes To—Early Morning

Flooded with whiskey's memories
again already arriving on lips

I shall not do this
wind horn sounding
body shaking

withdrawal's long slow language
Repeat the wolf's lies?
I am one thing not another
anger—the wolf—the danger
all the breath I will ever need

The wolf comes in on words—*I shall not*
The wolf has already eaten you
The drink's drink
Me—me—me
 capped under whiskey's full moon
the wolf's measure of wolfness—

wherever home opens
wherever the moon no longer holds power

a bottle's eye

I Am The Wolf's Unending Meal

What shall I tell you about the wolf? / Dark as a rush of thunder / as hungry as I At least / I thought / meeting in alleyways between bars / We dusted / A cold January The smell of the wolf's body turned me / over He smelled of earth / home / sweat and shit and all / great memories earth bears / with love There was not enough liquor / Never enough / Cold night / two bodies / in the dark / the promise of forgetting / for a moment / the jaws / of the animal that haunts you / A shame / Back home / not looking at the body / the wolf dragged in / Not recognizing / it was me

Hunted

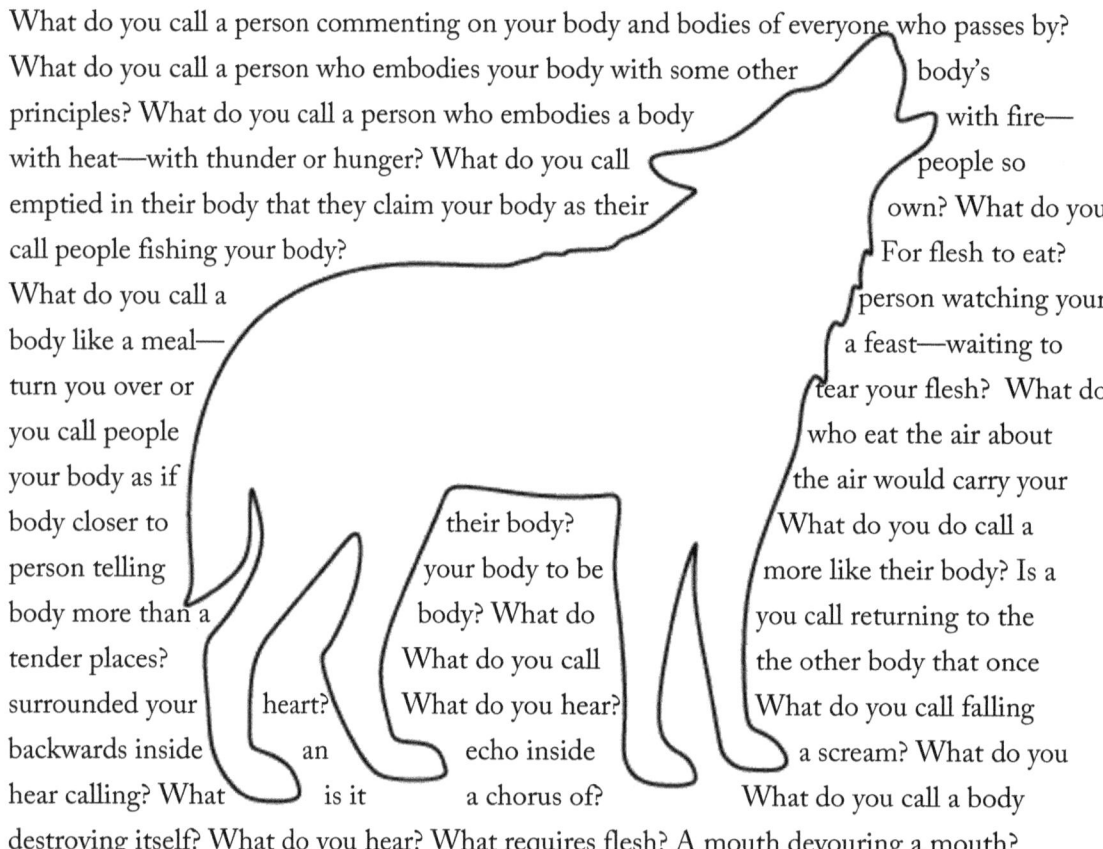

What do you call a person commenting on your body and bodies of everyone who passes by?
What do you call a person who embodies your body with some other body's
principles? What do you call a person who embodies a body with fire—
with heat—with thunder or hunger? What do you call people so
emptied in their body that they claim your body as their own? What do you
call people fishing your body? For flesh to eat?
What do you call a person watching your
body like a meal— a feast—waiting to
turn you over or tear your flesh? What do
you call people who eat the air about
your body as if the air would carry your
body closer to What do you do call a
person telling more like their body? Is a
body more than a their body? you call returning to the
tender places? your body to be the other body that once
surrounded your body? What do What do you call falling
backwards inside heart? What do you call a scream? What do you
hear calling? What an echo inside What do you call a body
is it a chorus of?
destroying itself? What do you hear? What requires flesh? A mouth devouring a mouth?

42

I Met The Wolf Halfway

at the elm taller than daylight
the way wildness can teach itself
learned on the hurricane bye
at first—the wolf learned
and lent its eye to the wind
and lent its wind to the hunger
and lent its mouth the eye
to understand what must be done
to find happy waiting

at the elm grown into its wildness
forgetful of wisdom
the wolf did not recognize me
with a mouth
and understood me that way
and lent its hunger to me
and lent its nose wisdom
so that I may flesh my own emptiness
inside

The Inside of a Wolf

I gut the wolf—All I find is a hole / and I follow / the hole farther in and farther / into earth shaped like a great sigh / The earth—open and airy / as sky The earth is blue / as thought inside— farther / and further—the wandering / into earth—until a great opening opens / up beneath the hole / and suddenly nothing has a body Nothing / has a body but me—Into the belly / of the wolf I fall—farther / and forward into emptiness Inside / the earth is blue Blue / is the absence of all / earth—all body—and I tumble into blue / so shattering—so empty / all body comes / back—a kind of courage—holding on to one's body—so / tight—while tumbling / and turning / into a sigh Holding on / to one's body so tight / all breath is lost Falling / into earth— so careless / with its emptiness—so daring / hiding inside a wolf—the moon's mouth

Mirror The Wolf

I split into two the wolf split into four we kept dividing our greatness

until I matched the air —the wolf matched the earth —both of us hummed

and harmonized with the song that kept reverberating through the world—

which was me—which was the wolf —I could feel the wolf in the wolf's matrix

—I could feel the wolf's fear the wolf's wonder and the wolf could see me

fine and true— together we continued to enlarge

emptiness which was inside us which was our container—emptiness

Patience— space—the end of the lie's lie

Wrestling With The Wolf

At times—the wolf's jaws lift   me

out of me and   back into the belly of the wolf

At times singing brings me out   of emptiness

At times—   —we are nowhere

unless rain falls and joins us   with all—meadow—blade—fiber

the rings' song   as it winds round

the pine—meadow—soft—forgiving   At times we wrestle in boughs

and in boughs we inosculate—   —we break again

in hurricane wind   and tumble over tumble

the wolf ripping—   and I know emptiness and emptiness

is all

   When I vibrate out and sing

sing—sing myself out—at last—   —borrowing happiness

from the moon—I borrow the space   between emptiness

and glow until my kind in green   and in growing

arrive and we sing together   The wolf retreats into emptiness

46

A Wolf Devours A Wolf Devours A Wolf

I devour the wolf so the wolf does not   devour me
I devour the wolf so the wolf does not   devour me

I place my hunger—outside the wolf

                               wolf—outside in the field

                so empty   the wolf wishes to devour emptiness

                               to increase

          the wolf's hunger

          there is a hunger
        in a wolf—to satiate   my own desire

        I swallow the hollow   I devour

        I place myself outside   myself
                               the wolf

I Make A Roof Out Of The Wolf

Eating   on its back—broken

racked—stretched   —propped up with bones coughed up

from a belly with no bottom   —the wolf belly

drinking from a skin of wine   that never runs out of thirst

It owns my home   old knowledge of the body—a home

Settled in softness   —waiting for softness to assume its body—

I make a roof out of the wolf   I brace its beaten fur

with its bones   — I keep my knowledge dry

I keep my knowledge free   from sun rot

The moon cannot find me   —sheltered by want

In Some Southern Village

Fuck the wolf / with the moon / squeezing borrowed light / into a screw / to undo the wolf / by attaching emptiness to emptiness to be full / Why can't you? / Be Full? / Fuck up the wolf with a pipe / of want—with a hammer wanting / Do not stop / til all teeth lay / like broken rocks / at the moon's feet / The wolf's mouth / full of the south / fuck the wolf / with a hand me down fist / from a generation back / that aches / and pines /and wants / to make the wolf scream / for the small feasts / the wolf made / and ate and ate / and then returned the next day / to gloat / about their emptiness / Fuck the wolf / with its own mouth / stretch it around / south to slide it up / the hole / where all its hunger comes out / to become hunger again / Fuck / The / Wolf

Diagram Of Transformation

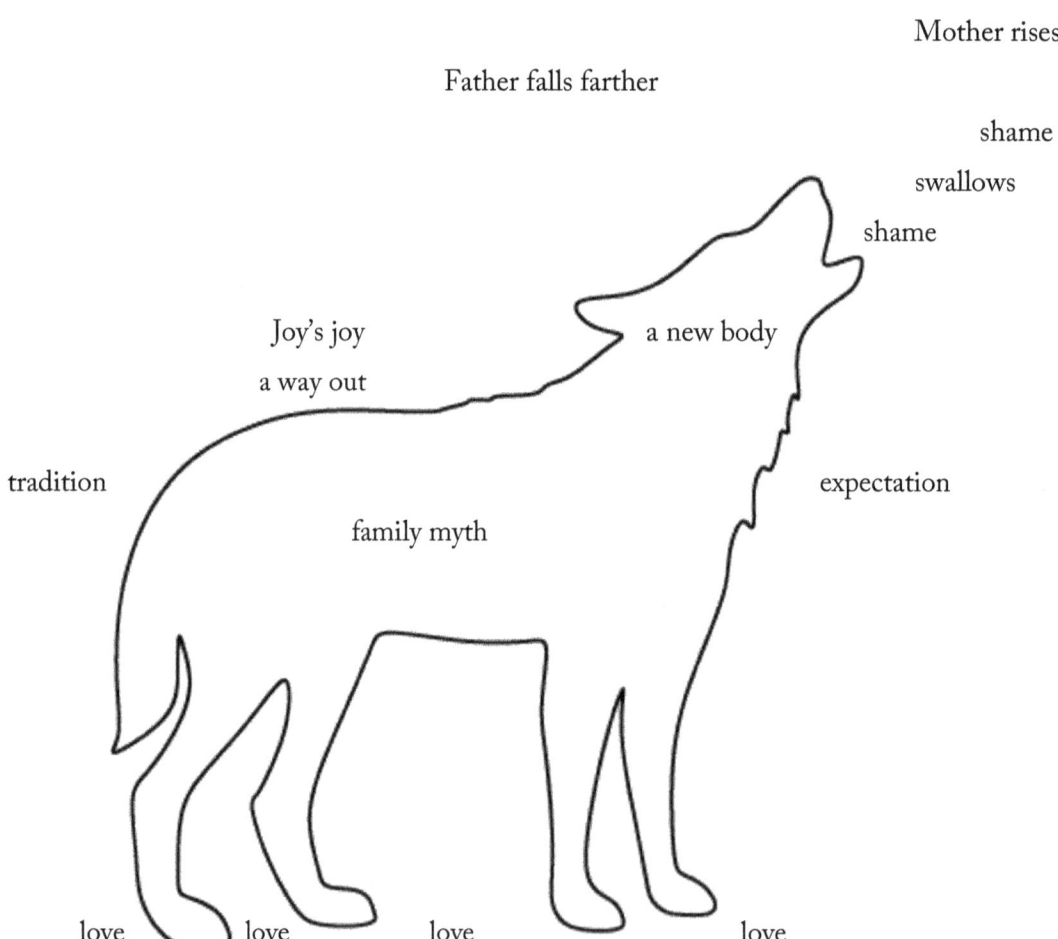

Mother rises

Father falls farther

shame

swallows

shame

Joy's joy

a new body

a way out

tradition

expectation

family myth

love   love   love   love

50

Wolf In The Meadow

Wolf celebrates emptiness / by making more emptiness The cold emptiness / of the moon's music is open open / What a great service to the moon / creating emptiness for the moon's influence

Why is it father wolf talks to the pup / through the moon? Why is it mother wolf shames / the pup through the moon? Who / is the moon to a meadow mind? Sunlight / is the riddle—pollen and dew its turns

The moon's mind / borrowed / from the sun's happiness / The wolf who is not a wolf knows this

Wild grain growing up / on the edge of some windlorn brace of locust / twisting up through the swamp's edge / here the wolf minds warm happiness / of the green—here the wolf is not

Wolf Who Is Not A Wolf Plays In The Forest

About the wide
lightning forked
trunk—wolf laid

I am here
I am—here
I am Here

moon comes out
but does not call
Ocean's oceans

Come to me
I'll care for you For you I'll be full
of emptiness—you

a pinecone
the moon
a life

a river stone
wishes to gobble up
Mother ocean

a jaw around flesh
Wolf shares fragility
with no one

Moon
moves further away
when wolves approach

borrows everything
Happiness
more—more—more

Moon—a rind

above the den—forest mind

turning over winter

Soft moments to learn

what it is to be alive

in wolf skin when it wants

to be a doe

cloverwild

free of anger

Inside The Hollow Is A Song

Voices called
—home
as empty—as the
a wolf
—do you hear?

My name leapt
—my singing high
—the wealth of laughter
rings inside
the wolf's menace—
Softness is forever

The chorus? *Mine mine*
—home—
bottom of emptiness
—I am one thing not another
There is a body now—isn't there?
All father diminished
through me
—my laughter high
—a liquor without a cup
inside my emptiness—emptiness
how could I not answer my name?
Softness Is forever

Do you hear ? A chorus clept
the moon empty
inside the gut of a wolf who is not
The chorus? *Mine—mine*
Ocean's ocean—time
all mother enlarged
—my name returned to me
—my mirth
A chorus of strings
I rhyme my emptiness with
The chorus? Do you hear?
Softness is forever—forever

Noctivagant

Wolf removes tail— enlarges it— swings
back to the old forest with it and waits
for owl to arrive with news Wolf
removes ears and pockets sound—turning
circles in the must of deadfall and shatter
while rabbit gathers rabbit out by the heather
Wolf removes mind forgets the moon's songs—

Come to me—father
Give all father to me—mine
All and what will be

Wolf removes nose and digs into earth—waits
for root—wending wise and through Wolf removes
eyes—shakes songs with fungus—the rooted valve
of tree—the rooted valve—a life Wolf removes
wolf from wolf and divides into hunger
calling for the mother of emptiness calling

All and what will be
Give all father to me—mine
Come to me— father

Wolf turns inside out towards mother—
becomes desire—hunger—which was all
the wolf learned—which was all flesh
was—hunger under the hunger—a mouth
devouring a mouth devouring a mouth

Father turns Into
mother all desire goes
Under love all waits

Wolves Prop Up The Moon   They Gather—Rhyming

and spring after each other	as quick as limed light
gifted from the moon	which is lifted from the day
like flesh is lifted from flesh	as night becomes what it chases
a cradle—a cradle	dreams
pollen gifted and gifted	by the tree
cast like cones	each further
farther	than the last
seven wolves	children of want—wanting
rushing—leaping—springing	from want
desire a lark in a morning tree	hunger—tomorrow—tomorrow
there is always	tomorrow
desire	chasing hunger
opening	a moon
I have a body	her name is happy
I have a body	their name is happy
the body of laughter	a flame to breathe a name
into a body	I have at last

Swallowed By The Wolf

Emptiness has me   emptiness has me
emptiness has me doubting   my emptiness
because emptiness   can fill up on emptiness and be full of itself

Emptiness   a glad hand
shaking hands with another   glad
hand   about the end—So what?

I borrowed happiness   to lift my emptiness up and out
with all father—so what?   Emptiness has me
The emptiness has me   The emptiness has me in a pinch

between a hole and   a space defined only by its emptiness
The hole–a rough–rocky throat   ready to swallow
Do I deserve to be   eaten up? Do I desire

to be   a part
of that emptiness?   A vast open place—to be
filled up again and again   again?

I sing—whistle   My voice sings back

a open wave from a friend   across the way

joy echoes back   echoes back echoes back

Emptiness Sestina

To fill my emptiness / I stole from the mouth / of the wolf / and took the happiness of the moon / to sate my hunger / to desire / what all spirits desire / a body to embody and rise out of emptiness / my hunger / to escape my body—a mouth / as open as the moon / to flesh and flesh and consume like a wolf / devouring a wolf / and doubling the desire / for the moon / and doubling the emptiness / and doubling the mouth / hunger's / hunger / all I know of my body passed from a wolf / the importance of a mouth / to enflesh desire / to diminish emptiness / by borrowing happiness from the moon / in doses Happiness borrowed from the moon / diminishes hunger / restless emptiness / of more more more wolf / and what the wolf desires / a mouth / devouring a mouth / in service to the moon / and a body's desire / to fill emptiness / A wolf / a hunger's / hunger—the wolf's emptiness shining like a moon in me

What The Wolf Fears

The spirit stirring inside— tossing their hair back

for the first time posing in the mirror

as satin slips over the knees the wolf discovering the body

wears the spirit—the spirit wears the body draped

in silk danger—silk nothings a man's idea

of a woman— lace trim—a choker—

garters and their hitch The sway—

satin cupping—rubbing the wolf's ends—the way satin glistens

slick with desire's desire to embody a body—

happy—to understand a body as it becomes

the body the spirit wishes to wear—a gift

the wolf gives to the wolf—mirror

returning softness to the interior—the mirror—not a mirror

but a door the other side bright

with laughter —a chorus humming—*here*—*here*—*find us*

here A body—a door

On The Four Corners Of The World

I put the wolf outside myself I put the wolf inside
The wolf Inside Me—the shaking denial Inside With me
Wrapped in skin—fur What shall happen? No hope—a claw
When I step outside this pack will I be prey? Clawed
Or shall I pray with the prey to be unfound? An exile
If I am unfound I shall find my own waiting from the moon's rhymes
There is a crossing I crossed it   I had to my own song for living   For love

In the moving—a wine glass hum The wolf inside knows
the vibration through the well
the center— I put the wolf outside
through stone—through wood to undo
wood—alone An idea what man has done
vibrating through a wolf I build a wall to keep the wolf
who knows they are not I build a wall to house
a wolf a woman—a man's not

Pelt Of The Wolf

For JAH

What a beautiful

idea—to sleep soundly

in a space surrounded by predators

Only a wolf can sleep

without remorse —without worry

in a forest Do not

forget

the wolf's body—so large
it eclipses all It is all
one can see—the wolf—dozing
by river's river—the wolf
romancing meadow scents

mine—mine—for my want

for my wicked emptiness

make emptiness—mine

The wolf

Eats The moon has sworn to it The wolf's emptiness

engulfs It is space

                                                            Without a moon—a space
                                                                         without

Hunting—pelt of the wolf I wear
it Tend to it—hang it up
with soft hands Its worth In the glamour
Hunting The wolf Wearing joyous glamour

                                                            We find each other Out

in wilderness—we catch
each other's eye We
match—blood hope

                    Through green into green and out
                        again—tracking the wolf
                            by scent and track
                            and scat—so many
                            familiars—signs
                    of predators preying and prey
                                praying

with deliberate action—for another
—for themselves—cleaning—preening
earth away away—shaking a leaf cup of rainwater
into the lips of another—what a prayer
it is to live The wolf deserves none
of this But serves it so the same

The wolf deserves none of serenity's silence

                              the noise of small bodies

                         moving at the edge of a forest

                              where the meadow preens

                         preens preens—look at me

                                        Some new danger

                                   already tears itself anew

                                   In this wood— moving

                         with quickening deliverance—a cardinal

                              sings A cardinal answers

                    Pay attention

                         Wait

                       Laughter

                 A returning call

The wolf's hide lays across
the floor The wood stove's wisdom
fading as it loses wind
—its declaration dying down
for a bit All around it—a family
of the river drinking tea
out of turned up flowers
tramping all over the wolf
—without thinking They spill joy

over the pelt—kick it—the snout

—a shriveled button that once snarled

no—now a toothless gum line—like a stray

hem turning up or turning down

the way the forgotten go—a picture

slipped from a frame—a cross

worn to the touch—a letter

dropped—a name that changed

I Dress the Wolf in Flowers

I go singing
in the park—
the park tidy with wolves

reading about flowers
on all the good benches—
in the park—while larks sing

in the park—lounging
the wolves—
freedom from hunger

I dress the wolf in flowers
by naming each a color
as I pass—

by naming each
as I go singing My name—bright—
A name has so much knowledge

a petal in the park
ringing—
of levity—weight—balance

No more anger—
it floated away
like a balloon

Even wolves lose all anger
without it—noses shriveled buttons—
without meanness

Wolves know slack
faces slack
Without anger

the wolves grow soft A tulip

sprouts from the head of a wolf—

an ear becomes flowering woundwort

Wolves grow drowsy   on benches—the park full

of wolves   blooming

The butterflies rouse colors—   a pair of doves settle

on a downy head of fur—

a dog turns without fear—

an elm shakes their feathery fingers—

behind me—   one by one

wolves slumber in green—   the green lending its memory—its joy

— in the moment—   in the singing

Acknowledgments

I would like to thank Richard Siken for his care in working on this project. I would like to thank Jennifer Harris and the JackLeg Press staff for their care with this book. I would like to thank the staff at *Great River Review*, where I first read poems from this project in the winter of '22. Two of these poems were inspired by listening to the Breaking Form podcast, "For The Wolf I Left" and "Pelt Of The Wolf". Many thanks to Nancy Mitchell and The Poet's Corner for supporting my work. A shout out to Sista Big, Amber Green, and Tara Elliot for all you do for the local poetry community. Thank you to Alexander Weinstein and the staff of The Martha's Vineyard Institute of Creative Writing for affording me a place to recharge and rework this manuscript. Many thanks to Melissa Onstad, Earl McBride, and Jake Zuppa for putting up with me during its completion. Many thanks to Rayne, Crow, Ginger, Sarah, Auntie Em, & Semok for support and love these last few years. Much love to Mom for being my cheerleader.

This book is for the march, for the ivy, for the thunder, for the love.

Conjunctions: "The Inside of a Wolf," "wolf moves in the shape," "Wolf In The Meadow" was
    published as "Wolf Celebrates"
Evergreen Review: "In Which I Address the Wolf," "Wolf in Dark Elms"
Foglifter: "Wolf Territory"
Texas Review: "I Dress the Wolf in Flowers"

The Bennington Review: "Wrestling with the Wolf," "On the Four Corners of the World"

Havehashad: "Halloween With the Wolf" was originally published as "All I Got For Halloween Is Candy"

Four Rivers Review: "Floor Plan"

Monocle Miracle: " Self Portrait", "Diagram of a Mother" was originally published as "Diagram of a Fairy Tale"

Mud Season Review: "Wolf Who Is Not A Wolf Plays In the Forest" was originally published as "Wolf Who Is Not A Wolf Plays Board Games"

Sho Poetry Journal: "Swallowed by the Wolf," "Mirror the Wolf" was originally published as "Queerness is Infinite"

South Florida Poetry Journal: "In Some Southern Village" was originally published as "Fuck The Wolf"

New South: "Seven Wolves Prop Up The Moon They Gather Like A Rhyme," "Emptiness Sestina" was originally published as "To Fill My Emptiness"

Cobra Milk: "Take One Mouth And Consumer The Other"

Night Heron Barks: "I Met the Wolf Halfway"

On the Seawall "Growing Up in the Mouth of the Wolf"

The Blue Mountain Review: "What the Wolf Fears"

The Comstock Review: "I Put the Wolf Outside Myself"

The Ilanot Review: "I Make a Roof Out of the Wolf," "The Wolf Eats"

The Mississippi Review: "Shelter of the Wolf"

Whale Road Review: "Wolf Promises of Love"

West Trade Review: "I Am the Wolf's Unending Meal"

Sonora Review: ""What Wolf That Kissed Me So" was originally published as "Kissing The Wolf"

"What Claims Wolves Made On My Body" was included in the anthology Mid South Sonnets, edited by CT Salazar and Casie Dodd, from Belle Point Press.

JACKLEG PRESS EST. 2018

V. Joshua Adams ✳ Mark Baumgartner ✳ Scott Shibuya Brown ✳ Michael Chin ✳ Chloe Clark ✳ Rivka Clifton ✳ Brittney Corrigan ✳ Jessica Cuello ✳ Barbara Cully ✳ Allison Cundiff ✳ Curious Theatre Branch ✳ Genevieve DeGuzman ✳ Suzanne Frischkorn ✳ Victoria Garza ✳ Reginald Gibbons ✳ Joachim Glage ✳ Caroline Goodwin ✳ Brett Hanley ✳ Summer Hart ✳ Kathryn Kruse ✳ Brigitte Lewis ✳ Jenny Magnus ✳ DK McCutchen ✳ Jean McGarry ✳ Rita Mookerjee ✳ Mamie Morgan ✳ Alexis Orgera ✳ Zach Powers ✳ Karen Rigby ✳ Jo Salas ✳ Maureen Seaton ✳ Kristine Snodgrass ✳ Cornelia Spelman ✳ Peter Stenson ✳ Melissa Studdard ✳ Gemini Wahhaj ✳ Megan Weiler ✳ David Welch ✳ Cassandra Whitaker ✳ David Wesley Williams

jacklegpress.org

www.ingramcontent.com/pod-product-compliance
Lightning Source LLC
Chambersburg PA
CBHW041150120626
46547CB00020B/3176